SuperStarters

Activities for Young Children

by Bobbye S. Goldstein
and Gabriel F. Goldstein

FEARON TEACHER AIDS

A Paramount Communications Company

Publisher: Virginia L. Murphy
Editor: Lisa Schwimmer
Illustration: Corbin Hillam
Designer: Diann Abbott
Cover Design: Marek/Janci Design

ISBN 0-86653-899-2

Printed in the United States of America
1.9 8 7 6 5 4 3 2 1

About the Authors

Bobbye S. Goldstein is a popular speaker and writer both nationally and internationally on a variety of subjects related to reading. A major portion of her career was spent as a reading specialist with the New York City Board of Education. She is a former Board Member of the International Reading Association (IRA) and a Past President of the Manhattan Council. Bobbye was a founder of the renowned annual Parents and Reading Conference sponsored by the Manhattan Council in cooperation with Fordham University at Lincoln Center and served as co-director of two of Fordham University's summer institutes. She is the recipient of the prestigious IRA's Special Service Award and was honored by Reading Is Fundamental with their Distinguished Volunteer Service Award. Her first book, *Bear in Mind: A Book of Bear Poems*, was an American Booksellers' Association Pick of the List. Her second book, *What's on the Menu? Food Poems*, was a 1993 Children's Choices selection by the IRA. Her third anthology, *Inner Chimes: Poems on Poetry*, was selected as a 1993 Teachers' Choices by the IRA, a Bank Street Selection for 1993, and a Best Book of the Year by Parents Magazine. Her latest anthology, recently published, is *Birthday Rhymes, Special Times*. Her first book with Fearon is the popular *Newspaper Fun: Activities for Young Children*. Bobbye lives in New York City with her husband, Gabe.

Gabriel F. Goldstein, a chemist by profession, worked for Interchemical Corporation (subsequently know as Inmont Corporation), a large manufacturer of inks and coatings. In the course of his career, he developed a unique set of inks for printing on plastic film for which he was awarded several patents. He traveled around the United States and Canada, as well as England, helping with the marketing of the company's products, including many of which he developed. He was a contributor to Chemical Abstracts, wrote articles for technical magazines, and spoke at professional meetings. After retiring from United Technologies, Inc. (successor to Inmont Corporation), he joined his wife in literacy efforts. *Newspaper Fun: Activities for Young Children* was his first book for Fearon. Gabe lives with his wife, Bobbye, in New York City.

. . . .

For our friend, Ginger Murphy
and our grandchildren, Jeffrey and Emily

B.S.G.
G.F.G.

. . . .

Contents

Introduction

Why *SuperStarters?*

SuperStarters is designed as a bridge between home and school. It describes activities that complement the school curriculum and encourages creative ideas to enhance early literacy. Its use by parents, teachers, and children will help youngsters get a meaningful head start with basic skills. Confidence in their abilities raises children's self-esteem and eases the transition from the freer atmosphere of the home or day-care provider to the more structured classroom setting.

Children learn through seeing, hearing, and touching. The activities in this book provide ways to use these modalities to advantage. They foster interest and enjoyment for the child as well as the teacher, parent, or caretaker. A positive nurturing attitude helps lead the way to success.

The ideas suggested here evolved from Bobbye S. Goldstein's more than thirty years with the New York School System and her subsequent extensive work, both nationally and internationally, on staff development, teacher training, and parents and reading.

Her workshops with parents and teachers have encouraged family literacy as a key factor in home-school relationships. In addition, her integration of trade books, poetry, and the newspaper into the whole language curriculum has been a model for replication.

Gabe Goldstein adds his expertise as an experienced writer and involved parent and grandparent.

SuperStarters will help give your youngsters a SUPERSTART!

Bobbye S. Goldstein
Gabriel F. Goldstein

Basic Concepts

Left Hand, Right Hand

Materials

- paper
- crayons
- pencils

As children develop independence in learning to dress themselves, distinguishing left from right becomes an important consideration. Some of the activities in this section help children remember which is left and which is right. Reinforcement through repetition is provided in a variety of interesting ways.

Give each child a large sheet of paper. Have children place their hands, palms down, on the papers. With a pencil or crayon, trace around the youngsters' hands and fingers. Label the hands *left* and *right*. Be sure to include each child's name on his or her work. Display the pictures in a prominent place.

Design a Pair of Mittens

Materials

- paper
- crayons
- blunt-edge scissors
- colored construction paper
- paste

Have the children place their hands, palms down, on pieces of paper. Draw around the youngsters' hands to create mitten shapes. Label which mitten is for the left hand and which is for the right. The youngsters can then color and decorate their paper mittens. If they wish, children can cut their mitten shapes out and paste on construction paper. Display children's work, being sure to include their names and the words *left* and *right* in the appropriate places.

Design a Pair of Bedroom Slippers

Materials

- paper
- crayons
- blunt-edge scissors
- colored construction paper
- paste

Trace the soles of each youngster's shoes on paper to make shapes for a pair of bedroom slippers. Label which is the left slipper and which is the right. Then have the children decorate their paper bedroom slippers with crayons. Help children cut out their slipper designs and paste them on construction paper. Display children's work, being sure to include their names and the words *left* and *right* in the appropriate places.

Make Up an Original Directional Poem

Materials

- oaktag
- hole puncher
- large loose-leaf rings

Make up an original directional poem and have the children act it out. Here's an example:

> Left, right, left, right
> Clap, clap, clap.
> Left, right, left, right
> Snap, snap, snap.
> Left, right, left, right
> Touch your toes.
> Left, right, left, right
> Touch your nose.

When doing this activity with the youngsters, be sure to stand facing in the same direction as the children to avoid confusion.

Make a collection of similar fingerplays to use with the children. Record the fingerplays on large sheets of oaktag and use with the children for review. Punch holes at the top of each sheet and keep the sheets together with large loose-leaf rings. This makes it easier to turn pages.

Teaching Left and Right Through Music and Fingerplays

Materials

- phonograph or cassette player
- records or cassettes of appropriate music

Play musical games, such as "Looby Loo" or "The Hokey Pokey," which emphasize the left and right with their catchy words and music. If you cannot play the piano, there are records and cassettes available featuring these popular songs. You may choose to just sing with the group. Children have a lot of fun doing these games and fingerplays.

Let's Have a Parade

Materials

- phonograph or cassette player
- record or cassette of appropriate music

To reinforce directionality, it's fun to have a parade. Play a lively march on the phonograph or cassette player. Children can march around the classroom in time to the music. Select a different child each time to lead the line. The leader calls out which direction to go—left or right. The children can have fun winding around desks and chairs. At home, children and family or friends can have a parade around the house.

As an alternative, select a child to be a traffic director. He or she can hold one sign that says *left* with an arrow pointing left, and another sign that says *right* with an arrow pointing right. As the leader and line reach a turning point, children respond to the traffic director's sign and turn in that direction. Children can take turns being the traffic director and the leader of the line.

Crowns

Materials

- oaktag
- construction paper
- blunt-edge scissors
- stickers
- pressure-sensitive tape
- crayons or markers

Children enjoy wearing crowns. They're easy to make and add a festive note to any occasion or parade.

Cut strips of oaktag or construction paper about three inches wide and at least 24 inches long. See that it is long enough for a comfortabe fit and a few inches overlap.

The children can decorate their crowns with crayons, stickers, and pieces of construction paper of varied colors. They can also cut points on the top of their crowns or leave the tops flat. Be sure the youngsters' names are on their crowns.

Place the crowns on the children's heads and fasten the ends together with pressure-sensitive tape.

Making a Flag

Materials

- lined or unlined paper
- construction paper (various colors)
- pressure-sensitive tape
- blunt-edge scissors
- crayons

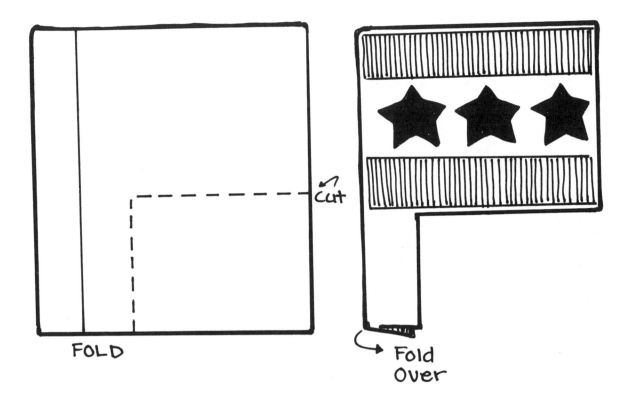

FOLD

Cut

Fold
Over

Children like to carry flags in a parade. They're easy to make and add to the fun.

To make a flag, take a sheet of paper and cut out a square in the lower right-hand corner. You may use lined or unlined paper. For a sturdier flag, use construction paper. Fold over the long part of the paper on the left-hand side several times to make the stick for the flag. You can strengthen the stick by wrapping pressure-sensitive tape around it.

Children can design their own special flags. It gives them the opportunity to be creative with crayons. After the parade, they can take their flags home to show their families.

Traffic Safety

Materials

- Phonograph or cassette player record or cassette of appropriate music
- black construction paper (8½" x 11")
- 2-inch red and green circles
- stapler and staples
- paste

Have each child make his or her own traffic light by folding a piece of black construction paper into four parts in the horizontal position, starting from the bottom. Place the two end folds over each other and staple the two together. Help each child paste a red 2-inch circle at the top and a green circle below the red. The children now have their own self-standing traffic lights.

To the tune of "The Farmer in the Dell," sing with the children:

> The green light says "go,"
> The green light says "go,"
> The green light says "go, go, go,"
> But the red light says "no, no, no."

As a follow-up to this activity, use the directional signs from the activity on page 22 for a safety parade. Using the back of the "left" and "right" signs, color one sign red and the other sign green. Designate one child as the traffic director and another as the leader of the line. Explain to children that the red circle means stop and the green circle means go.

Play lively marching music and have the youngsters march around the room following the leader, who responds to the signals of the traffic director. The line halts when the red sign is shown, and keeps marching when the green sign is shown. Children take turns being the traffic director and the leader of the line.

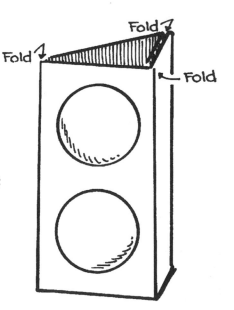

Big and Little, Large and Small

Materials

- paper
- oaktag or cardboard
- scissors
- paste
- crayons

Developing the concept of the correct size can be effectively implemented with the use of paper gingerbread dolls. Draw two gingerbread shapes— one large and one small. Draw two hats for the dolls as well, making one large and one small. Paste the gingerbread shapes and hats on heavy cardboard or oaktag and cut them out. Make a slit in each hat so that it can fit on the appropriate gingerbread doll's head. The children can then try placing the hats on the dolls. Have children determine the correct fit for each doll and then tell you why.

Extend the activity by making clothing for the gingerbread dolls as well. Then, with the children, try the clothes on the dolls, putting the wrong size on first to show that something is too little or too big. Then put the correct sizes on the dolls, showing how these are just right.

Nesting Cans

Materials

■ empty, round cans of varying sizes

To help children recognize size relationships, collect round cans of varying sizes that can nest inside each other. Be sure the cans are clean, have no sharp edges, and are perfectly smooth. Line up the cans by size on a table or desk. Have the children come up and point out which is the largest can and which is the smallest. Then remove some of the cans. Encourage youngsters to again point out which is the largest can and which is the smallest. Repeat this a few times with the cans in different line-ups, giving all the children a chance to take turns and participate.

In and Out

Materials

- paper plates
- long shoelaces
- hole puncher
- magazines
- crayons
- paste
- photos
- stickers

For each child, punch holes all around the rim of a paper plate. Have the children use long shoelaces to sew in and out of the holes around the plates. Make a knot at the end of each shoelace so that it will not come loose from the plate. Leave a small loop at the top so the plates can be hung on the wall.

Each child can decorate his or her plate with a photo, stickers, a drawing, or by pasting a picture in the center cut from old magazines.

In and Out Message Holders

Materials

- paper plates
- blunt-edge scissors
- long shoelaces
- crayons
- newspaper
- paste
- hole puncher
- clips

Children can make message holders using paper plates. Three paper plates can be used to make two message holders. Fold one of the paper plates in half and cut it on the fold. Place the half plate face down on one of the whole plates. Clip the two parts together and then punch holes around the circumference of the plates. The children can then sew the two pieces together with long shoelaces going in out of the punched holes. Be sure to knot the ends of the shoelaces when the children are done sewing. Children can then decorate their holders with crayons. Children can also cut letters from the newspaper and paste them on the message holders to spell out the names of family or friends!

In and Out, Over and Under

Materials

- construction paper (various colors)
- scissors
- paste

Children can weave with paper while also learning the concepts of over and under. For each child, make a frame by folding an 8 ½" x 11" sheet of colored construction paper in half. Draw a 1½-inch border across the bottom and leave 1¼ inches on each side. Measure and cut one-inch vertical strips across the sheet from the top of the fold to the top of the border. Unfold the paper and you will have a fine frame for weaving.

From another sheet of colored construction paper, cut one-inch strips that are 8 ½ inches long. You may want to use more than one color for the strips. Model for the children how to weave the strips of paper into the frame by going over and under the slits prepared. Alternate the sequence by starting on top for one row and underneath for the next. Demonstrate how all the strips will fall out if it is not done this way.

When the frame has been completely woven, paste down the loose edges. Label the weaving with the child's name and display in a prominent place. Older children can weave on cardboard frames with strands of wool.

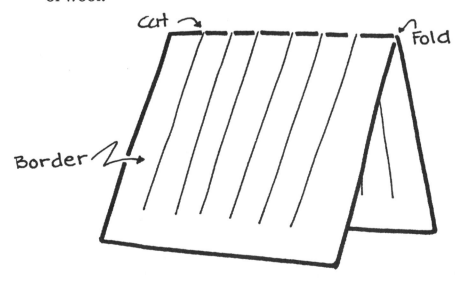

Responding to Directions

Materials

- props, such as a box, book, table, and so on
- paper
- crayons

Words, such as *over, under, in, out, off,* and *on* can be confusing to a young child just learning to follow specific directions. The suggestions here will give children experience in using these words. Model this activity with the children on a chalkboard or with crayons and paper.

> Draw a line under the flower.
> Draw a circle around the cup.
> Draw a line over the box.

Follow up by having some objects available that can be used hands-on. Ask the children to follow directions with various props. For example:

> Put the box under the table.
> Put the book on the table.
> Put the book in the box.
> Take the book out of the box.

Reinforce responding to directions by playing games, such as "Simon Says" and "Giant Steps."

Shapes

Materials

■ boxes of various shapes
■ *Boxes! Boxes!* by Leonard Everett Fisher

We are surrounded by different shapes. They help us recognize what an object is. Some of the basic shapes are identified here.

Read *Boxes! Boxes!* by Leonard Everett Fisher (published by Viking Penguin) to the children. Then display boxes of various shapes and sizes: square, oblong, rectangle, and round. Discuss with children what the boxes might contain. Demonstrate with props some things that may fit in each box. A long rectangular box might be for a tie, while a round box would be a good box for a hat.

Shape Reinforcement

Materials

- heavy cardboard or oaktag
- blunt-edge scissors
- crayons or marker

To reinforce shape recognition, cut out a set of large and small triangles, squares, rectangles, and circles from heavy cardboard or oaktag. Use these shapes as a demonstration model to discuss with the children. Prepare a similar set for each child. The children can color their shape forms with crayons or markers. Encourage children to match up their shapes to the demonstration model. The shapes are also useful as a reinforcement for big and little, large and small.

Let's Look Around

Material

■ drawing paper
■ crayons

After a discussion with the children about shapes, have children look around and identify the variety of shapes that they can locate right there in the room. The windows, the doors, a clock, and the doorknobs may be examples. The children can then draw pictures of their findings. Display their work on a bulletin board entitled "Let's Look Around."

Guess What's in the Box?

Materials

- food cartons of various shapes
- plain white paper
- tape

As a follow-up to other shape activities, bring in food cartons of various shapes. Cover the boxes with plain white paper so that the printing cannot be seen. Ask children to look at two similar box shapes at a time, and guess what each box shape is. Show the children how confusing it can be judging an object by shape alone. Explain to children that that is why there are labels with letters and words to identify items.

    spaghetti or waxed paper
    salt or cereal
    soap powder or rice
    whole milk or buttermilk

Let's Have a Party!

Materials

- construction paper
- paper napkins, cups, and plates
- plastic eating utensils
- fruit juice
- crackers, cookies, or cupcakes

Talk with children about setting a table for dinner or a party. A placemat is a rectangle, a plate is round, a napkin can be folded into a rectangle or square, and a glass is cylindrical.

It's fun to conclude a shape theme with a party. Each child can decorate a construction-paper placemat. When children add a paper plate, a paper cup, and plastic eating utensils, they're ready for a party! You can make it festive with crackers, fruit juice, cookies, or cupcakes.

Shape Pictures

Materials

- bags of paper circles and squares
- blunt-edge scissors
- paste
- construction paper
- crayons

At a teacher supply store and in many stationery stores, you can purchase bags of paper circles and squares. You can also cut these shapes out yourself. The shapes can be used to educational and artistic advantage as the children create shape pictures. The options are theirs, but here are some ideas:

boat	hamburger
turban	truck
building	flag
pizza	baby carriage
igloo	train

Sewing a Fruit or Animal Shape

Materials

- brown wrapping paper or a large brown grocery bag
- old newspapers
- crayons
- blunt-edge big-eye needles
- skein of wool

Sewing helps children use their small muscles and is valuable in developing their dexterity for writing.

On large sheets of brown wrapping paper folded over, draw the shapes of fruits, such as apples, pears, or oranges. As an alternate or at another time, you might want to draw teddy-bear shapes as well. Cut out the forms you have drawn. Place guide dots all around the perimeter of the shapes so that the children will know where to place the needle to sew the two pieces together. Then have the children color the fruits or bears.

Thread a large needle with yarn for each child. Show the children how to sew their shapes together following the guide dots. When the fruits or bears are half-sewn, have children stuff the shapes with strips of old newspaper. Then have each child sew together the rest of the fruit or bear. Display the finished fruits or teddy bears on the bulletin board.

For a large group, thread the needles and prepare the fruits or bears in advance. After the needle has been threaded, put the needle through the piece of wool so that it splits the yarn and makes a small loop. This helps avoid having to constantly re-thread needles.

Volume

Materials

- clear 8-ounce containers of various shapes
- 8-ounce clear measuring cup
- paper towels

To help children learn about liquid measurement, collect various 8-ounce containers, such as measuring cups, clear glass jars, and bottles of different shapes. Using transparent containers will help the children visualize that the same volume can be contained in different shapes. If you are using glass, be extra careful to avoid breakage.

Fill each of the containers with water. Then pour the contents of each container separately into a measuring cup and note how much water came from each container. The amounts should be the same, even though the bottles have different shapes. Keep paper towels handy in case of spills.

Making a Clock

Materials

- paper plates
- plain self-stick small circles
- markers
- construction paper
- paper fasteners
- wool or ribbon
- crayons or markers

Children generally have little trouble in recognizing numbers on a digital clock or watch. However, a traditional clock is more difficult. Children are often amazed, too, that people can tell time from a watch that has no numbers on the face just by looking at the position of the hands of the clock.

To help children recognize the spatial relationship of the 12 numbers on a clock, have them make paper-plate clocks. Give each youngster 12 stickers and a paper plate that has guide dots representing where the numbers should be. Draw a clock face on the chalkboard or on an oaktag chart as a model. Help children place the stickers over the guide dots. You can either pre-number the stickers or write the numbers with the children on their clocks. Punch a little hole on the top of each plate above the number 12. Tie pieces of wool or ribbon through the holes to hang the clocks on the wall. Make hands for the clocks from colored construction paper. Fasten the hands to the center of the clocks with paper fasteners. Children can bring their clocks home to share with their families.

Clock Dolls

Materials

- paper plates
- construction paper
- stapler and staples
- scissors
- self-stick circles
- paper fasteners

As a follow-up activity to making clocks, give each child another paper plate and 12 stickers. Have children place the stickers where the numbers of the clock should be. Some children may still need the assistance of guide dots to help them place the numbers in the appropriate spots. Have children fold strips of construction paper back and forth to make arms and legs for their clock dolls. Put hands on the face of the clocks with paper fasteners and attach the arms and legs with staples. Children can draw eyes and a mouth on the face of their clocks. Punch a hole in the top of each clock and attach ribbon so that the clock dolls can be hung on the wall.

Color

Make Up a Color Chart

Materials

- oaktag
- construction paper
- colored circles
- markers
- paste

On a large sheet of oaktag or construction paper, mount colored circles under each other. Write the name of each color next to the circle. Display the color chart in a prominent place until the children know and recognize both the colors and the color names.

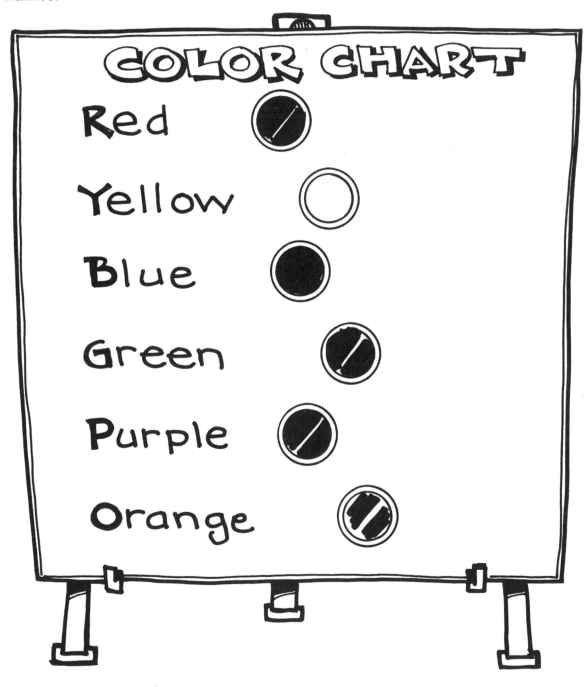

Make a Set of Colored Plates

Materials

- plain six-inch, uncoated plates
- five-inch colored circles
- paste

An inexpensive and convenient way to teach colors is to make a set of colored paper plates. They can easily be stored and stacked, or carried along on a trip to keep the kids entertained.

On six-inch undecorated and uncoated paper plates, paste a five-inch colored circle in the center of each. Use the primary colors first. They are red, yellow, and blue. Follow with the secondary colors— green, purple and orange. You may want to include black, brown, white, and pink as well.

Make up multiple sets of the plates so that they can be used in a variety of ways for color recognition, match-ups, and so on.

Reading from Left to Right with Color Plates

Materials

- colored plates
- pocket chart
- pointer

The colored plates (see page 66) can also be used to teach that in the English language, we read from left to right. Place the colored plates on the ledge of the chalkboard or in a row in a large pocket chart. Move a pointer across the plates as the children read the colors of the plates. The color plates are then rearranged. The children read the new order of the plates as the pointer is moved from left to right.

Playing with the Plates

Materials

■ assorted color plates

Give each child a set of paper plates consisting of one of each color (see page 66). Do not use more than six colors at a time for this activity. Have the children spread the plates out on their desks. Call out the name of a color. Each child holds up the plate that is the same color as the word called. At a glance, you will be able to tell who recognizes the color by the plate each child raises.

What's Missing?

Materials

■ various colored plates

To help children develop observational powers, play this game with the youngsters. Place six of the colored paper plates (see page 66) on the chalkboard ledge. Instruct the children to look at the plates. Then have them close their eyes. Remove one of the plates. Then ask the youngsters to open their eyes and tell which color plate has been removed.

Replace the plate on the ledge and repeat the process.

Learning to Recognize Color Names

Materials

- ■ strip roll or 5" x 7" cards
- ■ crayons
- ■ markers

Using strip roll, plain oaktag, or 5" x 7" cards, make up a set of color name cards. On each card, print the name of a color. Include a colored strip on both sides of each card for a clue to the color name. Review this with the children frequently. You can also have children match up these color cards to the color charts and color plates.

What's My Color?

Materials

- strip roll or cards
- colored circles
- pocket chart
- markers
- paste

Make up a set of cards with the name of each color on the front of the card. On the back of each card, paste a color circle that is the same color as the word on the front of the card. Place the cards in a pocket chart. Call children up, one at a time, to select a card and read the name of the color. After a child has read the name of a color, have the child turn the card over and see if the color matches the word he or she said. This is a self-correcting activity that the children can also play on their own.

A Crayon Poster

Materials

- oaktag or construction paper
- crayons
- paste
- tape

For variety, a crayon poster is fun to make with the children. Mount flat-back crayons on a large sheet of construction paper or oaktag. Place the crayons in a different arrangement from the previous color chart (see page 64) so that children will not rely on place or memory, but notice that the colors and words are in a different setting and order.

Find My Color Name

Materials

- chalkboard
- chalk
- eraser

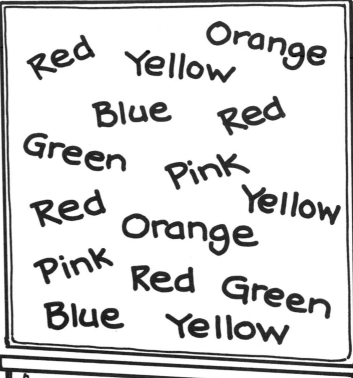

Write the names of colors randomly on the chalkboard several times. Say the name of a color listed on the board and call upon a child to come up and erase that color name. Repeat this several times, calling on different children until all the color names have been erased.

As an alternative to this activity, children who have already had a turn may say another color name and select the next child to erase the word.

How to Make Other Colors from Red, Yellow, and Blue

Materials

■ paper
■ crayons

Children will be interested in seeing how the primary colors can be blended to make secondary colors.

Help each child fold a sheet of paper into thirds, and then into thirds again in the other direction for a total of nine boxes. In the first box on the top left, have each child draw a red line, in the middle box a yellow line, and in the last box a red line. Then have children draw a yellow line over the red line. The yellow crayon line drawn over the red will change the color to orange.

In the second row of three boxes, have each child draw a yellow line in the box on the left, a blue line in the center box, and a yellow line with a blue line over it in the third box. The blue crayon line drawn over the yellow will turn the line into green.

In the line of boxes on the bottom, children draw a blue line in the box on the left, a red line in the center box, and a blue line with a red line over it in the third box. The red crayon line drawn over the blue line will turn the line into purple.

> Red + Yellow = Orange
> Yellow + Blue = Green
> Blue + Red = Purple

A Ziploc Glad Sandwich Bag can also show the youngsters how the blue and yellow strips look green when fastened together.

Making Bare Books

Materials

- white or colored paper
- stapler and staples
- manila folders or large envelopes

Children can make their own bare books. To do this, staple several pieces of white or colored paper together to form books. You may use any size paper, depending on the size of the book you would like. Legal-size paper (8½" x 14") makes a nice size book when folded and stapled along the crease.

Each child should have a manila folder or envelope to store the books-in-progress. Children can then work on individual books for several days until they are completed.

Making Flip Books

Materials

- 8½" x 11" paper
- stapler and staples
- blunt-edge scissors
- ruler
- pencil

An interesting variation on bare books are flip books. To make one flip book, take three sheets of paper and fold them in half. Then unfold the pages and draw a line across one page $1/2$ inch from the bottom. On another sheet, draw a line across the page 1 inch from the bottom. On the third sheet, draw a line across the page $1 1/2$ inches from the bottom. Then cut the sheets on the measured lines.

Put the three sheets back together at the center fold with the longest sheet at the bottom and the shortest on the top. Staple the three sheets together at the fold on the top and the flip book is ready.

Making a Color Book

Materials

- bare books
- old magazines
- blunt-edge scissors

Ask each child to select one color to make a color book. Using old magazines and catalogues, have the children cut out and paste pictures of that color in their bare books. A blue book would have pictures of blue objects, a red book pictures of red objects, and so on. Children can write "My Color Book" and their names on the covers.

Conduct a Color Survey

Materials

- ■ chalk
- ■ chalkboard
- ■ chart paper
- ■ markers

$\mathbf{A}$ color survey is an activity that can help children organize information.

Discuss the various colors of the children's clothing. On the chalkboard or on chart paper, list all the colors children are wearing. Then together with the group, tabulate how many youngsters are wearing each color listed, using a slash mark for each participant.

Celebrate Holidays with Color Bows

Materials

- construction-paper bows
- large safety pins
- construction paper
- blunt-edge scissors
- crayons
- paste

It's nice to have children celebrate special occasions by wearing a color bow appropriate for the day—red for Valentine's Day, orange for Halloween, and so on. For a large group, prepare the bows beforehand. Fasten the bows to the youngster's clothing with safety pins.

Older children can design and make their own bows using construction paper.

Let's Take a Trip to the Market

Materials

- crayons
- drawing paper

A trip to the fruit and vegetable market can help children learn and appreciate the wonderful colors of nature. Point out to the children yellow bananas, purple eggplant, red peppers, blue blueberries, and green cucumbers. As they go through the aisles, children will also be able to learn about green lettuce, orange carrots, yellow lemons, blue grapes, purple cabbage, and red apples.

After the trip, encourage the children to draw pictures about their visit to the market. Be sure that their names are included and that their artwork is displayed.

Making a Fruit and Vegetable Color Book

Materials

- bare books
- newspaper food sections
- magazines
- crayons
- markers
- paste

Give each child a bare book to paste pictures of fruits and vegetables that they find and cut out of newspapers and magazines. Help children write the name of each fruit or vegetable and the color of their selection. Children can write a title for their books on the covers.

The Colorful Fruit Bowl

Materials

- construction paper
- markers
- paste
- blunt-edge scissors
- colored squares of paper

Draw a large fruit bowl or basket on a 12" x 18" piece of construction paper. Cut the bowl out and mount it on a larger piece of construction paper.

Provide squares of paper in different colors for the children to use as they draw and cut out apples, bananas, pears, and other fruits of their choice. Children paste the fruits in the fruit bowl making an interesting collage.

Mount the fruit bowl picture in a readily accessible place so that the youngsters can paste the fruit on easily.

Numbers

Bounce and Count

Materials

■ large rubber bouncing ball

Bounce and count is a fun way to encourage counting skills. Together with the children, take turns bouncing a large rubber ball. Have the group count the bounces together. Ten bounces is the limit for each player. After every child has a turn, give children a second chance to bounce and catch the ball.

Make Up a Counting Song

Materials

- eleven 8 ½" x 11" cards

Make up 11 cards—the first card has one balloon on it with the numeral 1, the second card has two balloons with the numeral 2, etc. The eleventh card can say "And they all went POP!"

Together with the children, following the pattern of the song "One Little, Two Little, Three Little Children," make up another version of the song. Below are two examples. The children may want to suggest other words as well.

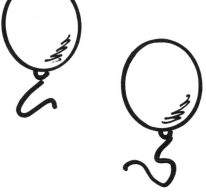

One little, two little
Three little balloons,

Four little, five little
Six little balloons,

Seven little, eight little
Nine little balloons,

Ten little balloons,
And they all went POP!

The song is sung together and everyone can clap at the word "POP!"

Another variation:

One little, two little
Three little bluebirds,

Four little, five little
Six little bluebirds,

Seven little, eight little
Nine little bluebirds,

Ten little bluebirds,
And they all flew away!

At the words "flew away!" the children wave their arms.

The Counting Song Poster

Materials

- construction paper
- oaktag
- paste
- markers

A poster provides reinforcement. Make up a poster for the balloon counting song on page 105 to help the children visualize the words of the song. Paste or draw circles on a large sheet of oaktag or construction paper for the balloons. Draw a string under each balloon. When singing the song, one child can be the leader highlighting the words with a pointer. This will emphasize the sound/symbol relationship for the group and the fact that we read from left to right.

> One little, two little
> Three little balloons,
>
> Four little, five little
> Six little balloons,
>
> Seven little, eight little
> Nine little balloons,
>
> Ten little balloons
> And they all went POP!

Coloring Balloons

Materials

- crayons
- drawing paper

Have the children draw pictures of ten little balloons in a row on sheets of drawing paper. Then have children color and number each of the balloons. Model this on the chalkboard before the children get started.

Explain to the children the difference in holding their papers in a vertical or horizontal position. The paper should be placed in a horizontal position for this activity.

Be sure the children's names are on their work.

Make Up a Counting Rhyme

Materials

■ 8½" x 11" cards

Following the pattern of the rhyme "One, Two, Buckle My Shoe," have the children make up another pattern rhyme with different words. The following is a suggested example.

> One, two
> What shall we do?
> Three, four
> Go to the store.
> Five, six
> Buy cookie mix.
> Seven, eight
> Cut, bake, and wait.
> Nine, ten
> Let's do it again.

The children recite the rhyme together as a group. At other times, ten children can perform in front of the class. Each child holds a large card with one line of the rhyme on it. The last line is said in unison. Encouraging children to participate in front of the class helps build their confidence in speaking before a group.

Number the back of the individual cards to help the children recognize where to stand when they say their parts.

Nursery Rhyme Cookies

Materials

- frozen cookie dough
- knife
- toaster oven
- cookie sheet

A tasty follow-up to the counting rhyme activity on page 110 would be to bake cookies with the youngsters. It is also helpful in developing patience as they wait for the cookies to bake and cool. Children learn that things take time.

Follow the directions on the package to make the cookies. Everyone washes their hands with soap and water before cooking, baking, and handling food. Children can help the grown-up in charge by placing the cookies on the cookie sheet and counting the number prepared.

REMEMBER: All activities that require baking, cooking, or cutting should be supervised by an adult. The handling of knives and all hot materials should be done only by the adult person in charge. Do not permit the children to handle any of the cutting or baking equipment, the toaster oven, or hot cookie sheets.

Make a Bead Board

Materials

- heavy cardboard
- 2 shoelaces
- 20 round beads in two colors, ten of each color

It's a good idea for children to have their own bead boards. It will help them develop their counting and number skills.

At a teachers' supply store, you can purchase boards on which to string beads for counting frames. It is also possible to make frames by punching holes in heavy cardboard.

You will need two shoelaces and twenty round beads, ten of each color, for each board. Help each child string ten beads of one color on one lace and ten beads of another color on the second lace. Fasten the shoelaces securely on the reverse sides of the boards so the beads won't come off.

The children can use these bead boards to count numbers by 1's, 2's, 3's, 4's, 5's, and 10's by moving the beads from left to right.

Matching Numbers and Objects

Materials

- paper
- crayons
- pencils

For each child in the group, fold an 8 ½" x 11" sheet of paper in half and then in quarters, making a total of 8 boxes. On the chalkboard or on a large sheet of newsprint paper, model how to draw simple items and label them according to how many of each item is in each box. For example, children draw 1 ball in the first box, 2 boats in the second box, 3 cars in the third box, and so on.

Any simple pictures can be used. The paper should be in a horizontal position. The children follow directions and copy the pictures and numbers that you model on the chalkboard. Remind them to put their names on their work. Display the results in a prominent place.

Making a Number Book 1 Through 10

Materials

- bare books
- colored circle stickers
- paste (if the circles and squares are not pressure-sensitive)
- large brown envelopes or folders

Give each child a bare book. On the cover, have the children write the words "My Number Book 1 - 10" and their names. Provide each child with colored circle stickers.

Model for the children how to put one circle on page 1 for the number 1. Do the same for each page, increasing the number of circles until you reach 10. Have children write the numeral and number name on each page.

On the last page, have the children list the ten numbers and write the number name next to the numeral. This activity is one that can be done over several days. A folder or large brown envelope with each youngster's name on it is a good way to store unfinished work. Keep the folders in a convenient place. When finished, the children can take their books home.

Different Configurations of the Number 5

Materials

- five pennies
- 8 1/2" x 11" cards
- markers

Help children become aware and learn to recognize that numbers can be put together in different combinations. Using pennies as an example, take 5 pennies and show the children the different groupings that can make up the number 5, such as two pennies and three pennies, or one penny and four pennies. You can do the same with 5 blocks, 5 toys, and 5 crayons. Make up large demonstration cards showing these number facts so they can be referred to by the youngsters for reinforcement and repetition. When you hold up the number cards, sing the number song about the different combinations that have been demonstrated. The words fit the tune of the song "London Bridge."

> Four and one are always five
> Always five, always five,
> Four and one are always five,
> We all know that.
>
> One and four are always five . . .
> Two and three are always five . . .
> Three and two are always five . . .

Repeat the refrain as often as necessary.

The Number 5 Book

Materials

- self-stick circles or colored circles and squares
- bare books (8½" x 11" paper, cut in half and stapled)
- paste
- crayons
- magnets

As a follow-up activity, children can make their own number books for the various configurations of number 5. Provide self-stick labels or plain-colored circles or squares and a bare book for each child. The number concept should first be modeled at the chalkboard by using five round magnets and having the children arrange them in different combinations.

When the children have internalized this concept, they are ready to make their own books. They can use the demonstration cards from the previous lesson as a guide for making different configurations of the number 5 for each page of their books.

Be sure to have the children include their names on the cover and the title "My Number 5 Book."

Learning About Doubles

Materials

■ 10 large blocks

To visually demonstrate the doubles concept, line up ten large blocks where the children can all see them. Start with 1 block and 1 block, which then makes 2. Proceed to demonstrate with the children the other doubles. Let them have a turn arranging 3 and 3, 4 and 4, and 5 and 5.

Making a Doubles Book

Materials

- 6-page bare books
- circles, plain or self-stick
- crayons
- paste

Children can make their own doubles books from 6-page bare books. Help children write "My Doubles Book" on the covers. A large-size version can be made as a model.

Use the inside cover and the opposite page for the first double spread. Have children paste one circle on each page. For the second double spread, children paste 2 circles on each page. Do the same for 3 and 3, 4 and 4, and 5 and 5.

To the tune of "London Bridge," teach the youngsters this song as you demonstrate the concept with your large-size version of the doubles booklets.

One and one are always two,
Always two, always two.
One and one are always two,
We all know that.

Repeat the song with the following words:

Two and two are always four . . .
Three and three are always six . . .
Four and four are always eight . . .
Five and five are always ten . . .

Let's Go Bowling

Materials

- large rectangular blocks or clean 2-liter plastic soda bottles
- large ball
- masking tape

A delightful way to reinforce number facts is to bowl with a big ball and large rectangular blocks. If blocks are not available, use clean, empty plastic soda bottles.

Line up the blocks or bottles in a row on the floor. Do not use more than ten. At an appropriate distance from the blocks, mark a line with masking tape where the bowlers are to stand. Have youngsters roll the large ball to the blocks to see how many they can knock down. Then have children count aloud how many blocks are still standing. Children take turns bowling and all count together.

This activity continues to help develop coordination.

Harriet the Chariot and the Wheels on Parade: A Play

Materials

- drawing paper
- crayons
- multiple copies of the play
- oaktag
- scissors
- markers

This play emphasizes ordinal numbers and rhyming. It also gives the children an opportunity to develop self-confidence in performing before an audience.

Provide the whole group with copies of the play. Children's parts can be written on separate cards made from oaktag for them to hold. Number the cards on the back so that children will know where to stand.

Assign roles to different children in the class. Perform the play for other classes, as well as a parent group. Children may wish to illustrate the different kinds of wheels.

Harriet the Chariot and the Wheels on Parade: A Play

Characters

Narrator
Dan, the Van
Gus, the Bus
Harriet, the Chariot
Kate, the Skate

Buck, the Truck
Michael, the Motorcycle
Ike, the Bike
Norma Jean, the Limousine
Molly, the Trolley

Whitney, the Jitney
Elaine, the Train
Moose, the Caboose
The Mayor

Harriet the Chariot and the Wheels on Parade

Narrator	Harriet, the Chariot, was president of the Wheels Club. Big wheels and little wheels were members. At their meeting, Harriet said "Let's have a parade this year." The others all agreed.
Dan	"I'll be first," said Dan, the Van.
Gus	"I'll be second," said Gus, the Bus.
Harriet	"I'll be third," cried Harriet, the Chariot.
Kate	"I'll be fourth," said Kate, the Skate.
Buck	"I'll be fifth," said Buck, the Truck.
Michael	"I'll be sixth," roared Michael, the Motorcycle.
All	First, Second, Third, Fourth, Fifth, Sixth
Narrator	A half-a-dozen of the members were ready. More wheels came to join the parade.
Ike	"I'm the seventh," said Ike, the Bike.
Norma Jean	"I'll be eighth," said Norma Jean, the Limousine.

Harriet the Chariot and the Wheels on Parade

Molly   "I am ninth," said Molly, the Trolley.

Whitney   "I'll be tenth," said Whitney, the Jitney.

Elaine   "I'm the eleventh," said Elaine, the Train.

Moose   "I'm the twelfth," said Moose, the Caboose. "I'm the last in line."

Narrator   The dozen members of the club were ready to roll. The parade was about to begin.

Dan, the Van, was first.
Gus, the Bus, was second.
Harriet, the Chariot, came third.
Kate, the Skate, was fourth.
Buck, the Truck, was fifth.
Michael, the Motorcycle, was sixth.

Ike, the Bike, was seventh.
Norma Jean, the Limousine, was eighth.
Molly, the Trolley, was ninth.
Whitney, the Jitney, was tenth.
Elaine, the Train, was eleventh.
Moose, the Caboose, was twelfth.

Up and down the streets they went.
It was a very exciting event!
People out for a stroll,
Stopped and watched all the wheels roll.

Harriet the Chariot and the Wheels on Parade

The mayor of the town was pleased and proud.
And he said so to Harriet and the crowd.

Mayor

That really was a great idea.
Let's have a parade again next year!

Reading and Writing

Getting Started

Materials

- newsprint or brown wrapping paper
- big crayons

The interrelationship of reading and writing has emerged as an important concept in developing early literacy. They go hand in hand as partners rather than separate entities. The three basic ways of teaching reading are the sight, sound, and tactile methods. It is beneficial to incorporate activities for each of these methods in a game-like situation. The activities suggested here are examples of just how closely aligned reading and writing can be and how they provide meaningful ways to move forward.

Young children enjoy sitting on the floor and writing on large sheets of newsprint with big crayons. It gives them room to spread out and use their large muscles. Provide this space in an uncluttered area where the youngsters can sit on the floor and scribble and draw.

Even their scribbles tell a story. Ask them!

Beginning Writing

Materials

- crayons
- pencils
- lined paper
- oaktag or strip roll
- markers

Scribbling is one of the first introductions to formal writing for youngsters. After this, they are ready for more controlled writing activities.

Make a large model of each child's name. Paste it on the youngsters' desks so that they will always have a correct sample in front of them.

Initially, children do best with thick crayons and big pencils. As they become more adept at writing, they can use thinner pencils and crayons. Providing lined paper is helpful as the lines add a measure of control. Lowercase letters take one space. Capital or uppercase letters require two spaces.

It is important for children to recognize that they need to leave a space between words. Otherwise, the letters and words will jumble together. The children will not be able to read what they wrote, nor will anyone else.

In most areas of the United States, manuscript writing is taught in the first and second grades. Cursive writing is postponed until the third grade. However, in Puerto Rico and other places, cursive writing is taught right from the beginning.

Painting on the Chalkboard with Water

Materials

- basin with water
- paper towels or newspaper
- chalkboard or slate
- paintbrushes

Children enjoy painting on the chalkboard with water. They can write words, names, and letters with their paintbrushes. As the water dries and disappears, children are also getting an interesting science lesson. They learn that the moisture evaporates into the air as the water on the chalkboard dries. Discuss this with the children and give other examples, such as the drying of laundry on a clothesline.

When playing with water, have newspaper or paper towels available for wipe-ups from spills.

Make Your Own Alphabet Sewing Cards

Materials

- heavy cardboard
- hole puncher
- shoelaces or blunt-edge needle and strands of wool

Draw large letters of the alphabet on sheets of heavy cardboard. With a hole puncher or tapestry needle, punch holes along the outline of each letter.

Give each child a long shoelace and demonstrate how to sew the letters, going in and out of the holes. A blunt-edge wide-eye needle threaded with a strand of wool may also be used. To prevent the wool from coming out of the needle after it is threaded, insert the needle through the wool strand to make a little loop. Then knot the end of the strand.

Always supervise sewing and cutting activities. For a large group, the needles can be pre-threaded.

Name Recognition

Materials

■ large pocket chart
■ name card for each child

Help children with name recognition by displaying the children's names in a pocket chart. Use the name cards for line-up time.

Select one name card and hold it up. The youngsters should be able to recognize their own names and line up. If they are experiencing difficulty, help them. The child selected chooses another name from the pocket chart for the next child. Each child has a turn to pick a name until all the children have been called up.

The names in the pocket chart are also helpful in taking attendance. The children can study the names in the pocket chart and tell you who is absent. Absentee cards can then be removed from the chart and placed in the absentee slot.

More Name Recognition

Materials

- chalk
- chalkboard

To give young children practice in recognizing their own names, write their names on the chalkboard, one at a time. Ask each child to line up for lunch or recess when his or her name is written on the board. Be sure to allow enough time for this activity so you are able to reach every child in the room.

Encourage children to practice writing their own names often. Explain to them that when they see the word *Name* with a line slashed through it, this means they are to write their own name and not the word *Name*.

Organizing Information

Materials

- chalkboard
- chalk

On the chalkboard, list the names of the children according to the first letter of each name. The children can consult the name pocket chart for reference. After the names are written on the chalkboard, count with the children which letter of the alphabet has the most names beginning with that letter and which has the least. This activity gives the children experience in organizing information.

Barry	Caren	Sarah	Tasha
Batya	Carl	Stephanie	Ted
Bernice	Charles	Sam	Timothy
Betty	Chuck		Todd
Blake	Cloe		Tyrone
Bonny			

Barry   Caren
Batya   Carl
Bernice   Chuck
Betty   Charles
Blake   Cloe
Bonny

6

Remember Your Name and Address

Materials

- bare books
- crayons
- large cards
- *Children's Songs: Songs of Friendship, Safety, Manners, Health* by Irving Caesar

It's important for young children to recognize and remember their names, addresses, and telephone numbers. They should also know their parents' names and the name of their baby-sitter, if they have one. Encourage parents to work with their children on this.

Have parents fill in the appropriate information in their child's own address book made from a bare book. Children can decorate their name and address books using crayons.

Then share with the children some of the songs in Irving Caesar's *Children's Songs: Songs of Friendship, Safety, Manners, Health* (published by Warner Bros. Publications, Inc.).

Family Album

Materials

- family pictures
- paste
- construction paper
- staples and stapler

Parents can make a family photo album along with their children. Paste photos of family members on construction paper. Write the name of each person in the photos and relationship to the child under each picture. Staple the pages together and add a cover page designed by the child.

Drawing a Family Portrait

Materials

- drawing paper
- crayons
- *I Got a Family* by Melrose Cooper

Read *I Got a Family* by Melrose Cooper (published by Henry Holt) to the children.

Have the children draw pictures of their families on drawing paper. Small families will fit on the paper held vertically. For large families, children will need to hold their papers in a horizontal position. Have children write their names on their work. Help the children, if necessary.

Help the children write the words *Mother, Father, Sister, Brother, Grandparent,* etc., to identify those in the pictures, if they wish.

Feely Letters

Materials

- ■ plain paper
- ■ sandpaper
- ■ crayons

Many children benefit from the touch as well as the sight/sound method of teaching reading. An easy way to make raised letters can provide the touch experience.

Have children place sheets of plain paper over pieces of sandpaper. Then with a crayon, each child can write a large letter or word on the paper. When the paper is lifted, the prickly surface of the sandpaper underneath will have given the letter or words written on the papers a raised texture. Try it yourself, too!

What Stands Behind You?

Materials

■ none

This is a simple take-turns game that both children and adults will enjoy. With your finger, trace a letter on a child's back. The youngster will then have to identify the letter you "wrote." Reverse the roles and ask the child to give you a turn and ask you to name the letter he or she wrote on your back.

Days of the Week

Materials

- 8½" x 11" cards
- paper crown
- *On Monday When It Rained* by Cherryl Kachenmeister

Make up seven 8½" x 11" cards, each showing the name of a day of the week. Number the cards on the back, with Sunday being number 1. Read *On Monday When It Rained* by Cherryl Kachenmeister (published by Houghton Mifflin) to the children. Then select seven children to stand in front of the room, each holding a "day of the week" card. Children use the numbers on the backs of the cards to help them stand in the correct order. The class then sings the following song to the tune of "Yankee Doodle."

> *Sunday, Monday, Tuesday, Wednesday,*
> *Thursday, Friday, Saturday;*
> *We are the seven days of the week,*
> *the seven days of the week!*

The child who is holding the card for the current day steps forward and says "Today is _____." The child holding the previous day's card says "Yesterday was _____." The child holding the next day's card says "Tomorrow will be _____." The child holding the current day's name card can wear a paper crown.

Days of the Week Board

Materials

- cardboard frame
- round bead
- shoelace
- markers

Using a cardboard frame, string a shoelace across the middle with one round bead on it. Tie the shoelace securely in the back so the bead won't fall off. Above the shoelace, write the names of the days of the week. Select a child to move the bead to the name of the current day. Make sure each child in the class will be given a chance. This activity should be done daily in conjunction with the days of the week song (page 163).

Months of the Year Song

Materials

- oaktag
- markers
- *Chicken Soup with Rice: A Book of Months* by Maurice Sendak

On 8½" x 11" sheets of oaktag, write the name of each month. Number the cards on the back with January as number 1 and December as number 12.

At the start of every new month, have the children sing the song that follows to the tune of "Yankee Doodle."

> *January, February, March, and April,*
> *May, June, July, and August.*
> *September, October, November, December,*
> *We are the twelve months of the year.*

Repeat the song frequently. Select 12 children to stand in front of the room, each holding a month card. If you have a large class, repeat the song with another group of 12.

The child holding the current month's card says the name of the current month. The child holding the previous month's card says the name of the previous month. The child holding the card of the following month steps forward to say the name of that month. The children can all sing the names of the month song again in unison.

You can also share with the children *Chicken Soup with Rice: A Book of Months* by Maurice Sendak (published by HarperCollins).

Word Families

Materials

- construction paper or index cards
- crayons or markers
- *Meet the Family Short Vowels* and *Meet the Family Long Vowels* by Bobbye S. Goldstein

Read *Meet the Family Short Vowels* and *Meet the Family Long Vowels* by Bobbye S. Goldstein (published by Andover Publications).

Word families are an effective way to encourage knowledge of the sound/symbol relationship. To develop this phonemic awareness, short and long vowel words can be printed on cards for the children. Put each word family on a separate card for each child. When the children have mastered the short vowel family, move on to the long vowel sounds.

Short vowel key words

| cat | pet | pin | pot | cut |
| bat | set | tin | cot | but |

Long vowel key words

| pale | meet | pine | cold | use |
| sale | feet | line | bold | fuse |

Palindromes

bun   nub
eve   eve
eye   eye
keep   peek
mom   mom
noon   noon
pit   tip

Materials

- junior or picture dictionary
- *Go Hang a Salami, I'm a Lasagna Hog! and other Palindromes* by Jon Agee

Read *Go Hang a Salami, I'm a Lasagna Hog! and other Palindromes* by Jon Agee (published by Farrar, Straus & Giroux). Then explain to the children that *palindromes* are words that can be read from left to right as well as right to left. Together with the children, see how long a list you can compile. You may want to encourage children to use a picture dictionary or junior dictionary for help.

bun	nub
eve	eve
eye	eye
keep	peek
mom	mom
noon	noon
pit	tip
pop	pop
pot	top
pup	pup
tap	pat
wow	wow

Using Old Playing Cards

Materials

- old playing cards
- pressure-sensitive labels
- markers
- small file box

Children enjoy collecting cards. Make this a learning experience. Using old playing cards, place plain pressure-sensitive labels over the face of each card. Write a reading or spelling word on each card. Encourage children to use the cards to practice their words. When children easily recognize each word, place fresh labels on top and supply new words or facts.

If children wish to save the cards as resources, the cards can be filed in a small box in alphabetical order.

Let's Go Fishing

Materials

- basin
- chalkboard pointer
- magnet
- scissors
- string

- oaktag
- paper clips
- pressure-sensitive tape
- marker

To reinforce words you want the children to remember, play "Let's Go Fishing." Cut out fish shapes from oaktag and write a word on each fish. Then secure a paper clip with pressure-sensitive tape on the reverse side of each fish.

Use a basin as the fish pond. Fasten a string with a magnet on the end to a chalkboard pointer. Children go fishing for words by trying to catch the "fish" with the magnet at the end of the string. Once children catch a "fish" word and recognize the word written on it, they keep the fish. If children miss the word, they are told the correct word, but the fish goes back into the basin. The child with the most fish wins. Be sure each child has several turns.

Wordless Picturebooks

Materials

■ wordless picturebooks, such as *Flicks* by Tomie dePaola, *The Sticky Child* by Malcolm Bird, *First Snow* and *Picnic* by Emily Arnold McCully

Many people are surprised to see a picturebook without words. They wonder why there are no words. The explanation is that the pictures tell the story.

Wordless picturebooks help encourage vocabulary and oral language in children. The stories become vehicles for retelling and develop the readers' sense of sequence and story.

Share wordless picturebooks with the children, such as *Flicks* by Tomie dePaola, *The Sticky Child* by Malcolm Bird (both published by Harcourt Brace Jovanovich), and *First Snow* and *Picnic* by Emily Arnold McCully (published by Harper Collins). Encourage children to "tell" you the stories as they look at the pictures.

Picture Stories

Materials

- old magazines
- construction paper
- paste
- blunt-edge scissors
- markers or crayons

Together with the children, look through magazines for colorful pictures that tell a story. It could be a child at the circus or a picture of someone eating an ice-cream cone. Have the children paste their pictures on construction paper and help them print the main thought of the picture under it. Display the pictures and discuss them with the group. This will help children develop vocabulary and a sense of story and sequence. Change the pictures frequently.

Add-a-Page

Materials

- construction paper
- hole puncher
- large loose-leaf rings
- old magazines
- blunt-edge scissors

As a follow-up to the Picture Stories activity on page 178, collect the picture stories that have already been displayed and put them together to make a class big book. This big book of picture stories should be left in a convenient place so that the youngsters can go back and look at it again and review the stories under each picture. Children can add pages to the big book. It can be entitled "The Add-a-Page Book."

House of Cards

Materials

- index cards
- blunt-edge scissors
- markers

There are many words that the children will have to remember by sight. To reinforce these words, it's fun to make a game out of it. By making word cards (5" x 7") with the words you want to review written on them, you have props for a good game.

Cut a 2-inch horizontal slit from the top of each of the word cards. The children select two word cards. If they say the words on the two cards correctly, they can make a house by sliding one card into the other and then standing them up. The child with the most sets wins the game.

Going Marketing with the Newspaper

Materials

- food section of the newspaper
- regular paper or construction paper
- paste
- blunt-edge scissors
- markers
- *What's on the Menu? Food Poems* selected by Bobbye S. Goldstein

Share some of the food poems with the children from *What's on the Menu? Food Poems* selected by Bobbye S. Goldstein (published by Viking).

Then fold two 8½" x 14" sheets of paper in half and then in quarters, making a total of 16 boxes on each page. Since only 26 boxes are needed for the alphabet, the six extra boxes can be used for overflow words. In each box, write a letter of the alphabet and then staple the sheets together. Have the children look through the weekly food advertisements in the newspaper and cut out the names of foods. The children then paste the food words in the boxes with the same initial letters as the food words they cut out of the newspaper.

It's fun for the children to compare the numbers of foods listed in each box. They can highlight the letter that has the most food words listed. Different foods are popular and in season at various times of the year. Therefore, the chart will have some changes every time you do this activity.

Collectors' Items

Collecting Leaves

Materials

- leaves
- light-sensitive paper
- crayons
- construction paper
  or drawing paper
- paste
- *ABCedar: An Alphabet of Trees* by
  George Ella Lyon

One way to help develop children's observational powers is to take a nature walk. This is especially appropriate in the fall when children can collect leaves. The *ABCedar Book* by George Ella Lyon (published by Orchard Books) has pictures of leaves from A to Z. Children can examine the leaves they collect carefully, noting the distinctive shapes and markings. Help children mount their leaves on light-sensitive paper. After a day or two, remove the leaves from the paper. The outlines of the leaves will remain on the papers. Be sure to have the youngsters put their names on their pictures. Display them on a bulletin board.

Leaf Pictures

Materials

- leaves
- construction paper
- crayons
- paste

After taking a nature walk in the fall, children can make pictures with the leaves they have collected. Have the children mount leaves on construction paper and draw around them. Some unusual and imaginative designs result from this. Display children's work for an attractive fall exhibit.

Stamp Collecting

Materials

- stamps from old letters
- construction paper
- blunt-edge scissors
- paste
- envelopes
- glassine envelopes

Stamp collecting can become a fascinating hobby. You can help the children become interested by carefully tearing off stamps and postmarks from letters both you and the children receive. Trim the stamps, but do not cut the perforations on the border of each stamp. Store used stamps in envelopes. Unused stamps should be kept in glassine envelopes.

To make this project more meaningful, children can look up information in the dictionary and encyclopedia about stamps. Discuss with the children any information they find.

Note:
The United States Post Office has several interesting pamphlets that encourage stamp collecting. Philatelic Centers are located in most main Post Offices of the larger cities. Introduction to stamp collecting, catalogues, and other materials are available from:

Philatelic Fulfillment Service Center
United States Postal Service
Box 44997
Kansas City, MO 64144-9997
Phone: 816-455-0970

More About Stamp Collecting

Materials

■ used stamps

Together with the children, establish categories to help sort the stamps. Stamps can be arranged by subjects, such as famous people, geographic landmarks, love, flowers, states, transportation, and so on. Children enjoy making albums for each category.

These categories provide a good avenue for looking up information in reference materials about the stamps' history.

This inexpensive, exciting hobby is an ongoing activity. It's also a good use for used stamps.

Make Your Own Stamp Album

Materials

- used stamps
- construction paper
- paste
- stapler and staples

Help children sort and arrange stamps according to their monetary value. Use a separate page for each denomination. How many varieties of the stamps can they find? How do the pictures differ? Help children make their own stamp books out of blank sheets of construction paper. Staple the pages together but do not staple the stamps. Use paste.

Design a Stamp

Materials

- drawing paper
- crayons

Children enjoy the opportunity to design their own stamps. Give them sheets of drawing paper on which to draw their own ideas for stamps. Have the children write their names on their work and display the results on a bulletin board entitled "Our Stamps."

Collecting Postmarks

Materials

- postmarks
- map of the United States
- world map, if postmarks are from overseas
- road map

Have the children bring in postmarks as well as stamps. It will become an interesting lesson in geography and map skills. Have children paste the postmarks in bare books. Children can each make their own postmark book.

Help the children locate the place on the map from where the letters were sent by noting the words on the postmark. Use the globe, regional maps in an atlas, or local maps.

Let's Find Out

Three-Letter Animals

Materials

■ picture dictionaries and encyclopedias

It is important to help children learn how to seek out specific information from reference materials. For young children, a picture dictionary is useful. Older children can use a junior dictionary. A junior encyclopedia is also a helpful book. A one-volume junior encyclopedia is less costly than a multi-volume set, and provides enough information for young children. Check them out in your local or school library before purchasing one for home use to see if it meets your needs.

Have children look through the pages of a picture dictionary or junior encyclopedia and locate animals that have only three letters in their names. Make an alphabetical list of the words on the chalkboard. Read about the animals with the children.

ape	dog	owl
bat	eel	pig
cat	emu	rat
cow	fox	yak

Four-Letter Animals

Materials

■ picture dictionaries and encyclopedias

Following the procedure for three-letter animal names, have the children look through the pages of a picture dictionary or junior encyclopedia and find animals that have only four letters in their names. Make an alphabetical list of the words on the chalkboard. Read about the animals with the children.

bear	fish	lion
bird	goat	swan
crab	gull	wolf
deer	hare	dodo
hawk	duck	kiwi

A visit to the zoo or wildlife conservation park, if one is in the area, would be a fine extension for this and the previous activity.

Making an Animal Scrapbook

Materials

- old magazines
- newspapers
- construction paper
- paste
- blunt-edge scissors
- stapler and staples
- crayons

Together with the children, look through old magazines and locate pictures of some of the three- and four-letter animals on the lists made in the activities on pages 204 and 206. Children may also find animal pictures in the newspaper and in advertisements. Help children cut out the pictures with blunt-edge scissors and paste them on pieces of construction paper. Label the names of the animals on the pages. Have the children design their own covers for their animal picture scrapbooks. Staple the pages of the books together. Be sure the children's names are on the covers.

Making an Animal Mural

Materials

- a large sheet of construction paper
- drawing paper
- crayons
- paste
- blunt-edge scissors
- masking tape

With masking tape, mount a large sheet of construction paper on a wall to serve as a background for an animal mural. Place it where children can comfortably reach. Have the children draw animals, trees, etc., on separate sheets of paper. With blunt-edge scissors, children can cut out their pictures and paste them on the construction paper to make an animal mural. This can be an ongoing activity.

Three-Letter Words About You

Materials

- chalkboard and chalk
- chart paper and markers
- paper
- crayons

Brainstorm with the children names of body parts that have three letters. Suggest that children refer to the dictionary or encyclopedia if they need help in finding words. List the body part words on the chalkboard or on chart paper as the children name them.

arm	leg	eye	ear
hip	rib	toe	gum
lip			

Have children indicate which words are part of the head and which are part of the body. Write children's ideas on the chalkboard. Extend this activity by having children draw self-portraits. Be sure their names are on their pictures. Display the artwork.

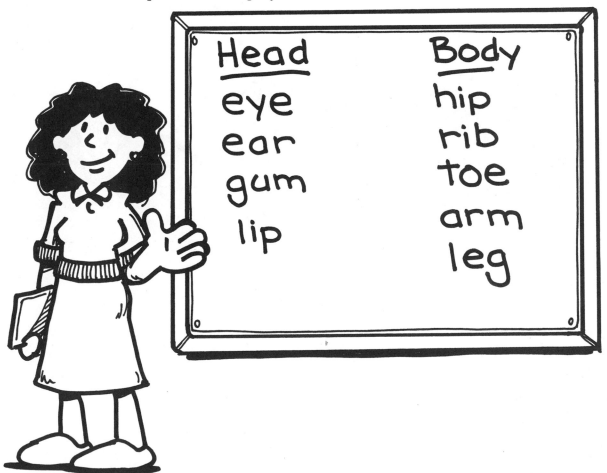

Hats, Hats, Hats

Materials

- old newspapers and magazines
- paste
- markers or crayons
- construction paper
- blunt-edge scissors
- *Caps for Sale* by Esphyr Slobodkina

Hats give us a clue to the kind of work a person does. Read *Caps for Sale* by Esphyr Slobodkina (published by HarperCollins) with the children. Then have the children look through the newspapers and old magazines to find pictures of people wearing different hats. Ask children to find hats for the following people:

> chef
> police officer
> firefighter
> sailor
> soldier
> construction worker
> mail carrier
> baseball player

Help the children make a hat scrapbook labeling which hat goes with each community helper. Discuss the kinds of work these people do.

A visit to the Post Office or Fire Department is an interesting experience for youngsters, too.

Play Ball!

PLAY BALL

Baseball
Basketball
Bowling
Football
Ping-pong
Tennis
Volleyball

Materials

- picture dictionary and encyclopedia
- paper
- crayons
- construction paper
- paste

Children can look through a junior encyclopedia or a picture dictionary to find sports that require the use of a ball. Then ask them to help you make an alphabetical listing of these sports on the chalkboard or on chart paper. Here are some examples:

baseball
basketball
bowling
football
ping-pong or table tennis
tennis
volleyball

Ask children to bring to school examples of different types of balls. This makes an interesting sports display.

Have children draw pictures of these different kinds of balls and label them. Mount the pictures on construction paper and display in the classroom.

Sports Scrapbook

Materials

- construction paper
- newspapers and magazines
- blunt-edge scissors
- paste
- stapler and staples

Ask the children to find pictures in the sports pages of the newspaper and in old magazines about sports games and athletes. They can cut out and paste the pictures on construction paper. Help children write appropriate captions under each picture. They can highlight one sport or do a compilation of many sports in their scrapbooks. Staple the pages together. Remind the children to put their names on their work.

Salt and Ice

Materials

- two clear plastic or glass containers
- ice-cubes
- salt
- clock or watch

Ask children if they know why salt is poured on icy streets. Explain that the salt reduces the time it takes for ice and snow to melt. This phenomenon demonstrated at home or in class.

Take two ice-cubes from the refrigerator and place each one in a clear glass or clear plastic container. Pour a tablespoon of salt on one cube in one of the containers. Leave the other cube alone. Clock the length of time it takes for each cube to melt. The cube with the salt on it will melt faster.

Observing the Clouds

Materials

- blue construction paper
- drawing paper
- crayons
- white paper
- paste
- blunt-edge scissors
- *The Cloud Book* by Tomie dePaola

Tell the children to look up at the sky and see the many types of clouds. Have them describe what they think the clouds look like. *The Cloud Book* by Tomie dePaola (published by Holiday House) is a useful resource. Call the children's attention to how the sky and clouds look before a storm. Encourage them to draw pictures of the sky and clouds. As a variation from plain drawing, have children cut out clouds from white paper and paste them on blue construction paper.

The Moon

Materials

- a current newspaper
- drawing paper
- crayons
- *Let's Read-And-Find-Out* books

- *Marcella and the Moon* by Laura Jane Coats
- *Birthday Rhymes, Special Times* by Bobbye S. Goldstein

The cycles of the moon are intriguing. Have the youngsters look at the weather page of the newspaper with you for the dates of the new moon, half moon and full moon. Ask parents to watch the moon with their children. *Marcella and the Moon* by Laura Jane Coats (published by Macmillan) is a good introduction to this activity. Read the poem "The Old Man Moon" by Aileen Fisher in the anthology *Birthday Rhymes, Special Times* by Bobbye S. Goldstein (published by Doubleday).

After reading about the moon, children can draw moon pictures. For additional information, books in the "Let's-Read-And-Find-Out" series published by HarperCollins are excellent resources.

Suggestions and Conclusion

Suggestions

Save the fun pages and any children's sections from newspapers and magazines in a special file for rainy-day activities. You and the children will both be glad you did.

Have a box or basket for the supplies the children will need to implement the suggestions in this book. A shopping bag is useful for holding extra newspapers, pictures, and magazines. Put the youngsters' names on their boxes and bags. This way, they will know which is their very own supply kit, always ready and available for them to use.

Supplies you will find helpful include:

newspapers, cartoons, and comic strips

old magazines with pictures

blunt-edge scissors

paste or paste stick

pencils and thick crayons

felt markers of various colors

drawing paper

construction paper of various colors

paper plates

brown paper grocery bags

oaktag or cardboard

plain envelopes

hole puncher

clips and paper fasteners

stapler and staples

yarn and string

pressure-sensitive tape

pressure-sensitive clear film

graph paper

oaktag strip roll

ruler

masking tape

loose-leaf rings

long shoelaces

self-stick circles and squares

$\frac{1}{2}$-inch and 5-inch circles

More Suggestions

1. Allocate a special time to work together with the children.

2. Do one activity at a time.

3. Curtail sessions if the youngsters become restless.

4. Provide a special place to store children's work. A folder, box, or basket can keep things readily available.

5. Arrange a display area, such as the refrigerator door or a closet door.

6. Review and repeat each concept as you go through the book, if you feel reinforcement is necessary.

7. Use the recommended trade books, rhymes, poems, and songs, as well as the newspaper, as resources.

8. Take time to read together every day.

9. Discuss things with each other.

10. Really listen and respond to what your youngsters have to say.

11. Try to write together at least once or twice a week.

12. Most of all, take time to enjoy doing these activities together with your children.

REMEMBER: YOUNG CHILDREN'S ACTIVITIES SHOULD ALWAYS BE SUPERVISED.

Conclusion

Early childhood is a very special time in a child's life with implications for future performance. A meaningful program of activity can provide the "super start" to help our children have a wonderful future. ■

Bibliography

Children's Books

Butterworth, Nick. *Busy People*. New York, NY: Candlewick Press, 1986.

Carlson, Nancy. *I Like Me*. New York, NY: Viking Penguin, 1988.

Clifton, Lucille. *Three Wishes*. New York, NY: Doubleday, 1992.

Cohen, Miriam. *No Good in Art*. New York, NY: Greenwillow Books, 1980.

Grejnieo, Michael. *What Do You Like?* New York, NY: North-South Books, 1992.

Hazen, Barbara Shook. *Tight Times*. New York, NY: Puffin, 1979.

Johnson, Angela. *One of Three*. New York, NY: Orchard Books, 1991.

Johnson, Dolores. *What Will Mommy Do When I'm at School?* New York, NY: Macmillan, 1990.

Modesitt, Jeanne. *Sometimes I Feel Like a Mouse*. New York, NY: Scholastic, 1992.

Moss, Marissa. *Regina's Big Mistake*. Boston, MA: Houghton Mifflin, 1990.

Pfister, Marcus. *The Rainbow Fish*. New York, NY: North-South Books, 1992.

Wells, Rosemary. *Noisy Nora*. New York, NY: Dial Books, 1973.

Basic Concepts

Burningham, John. *First Steps*. New York, NY: Candlewick Press, 1985.

Ehlert, Lois. *Circus.* New York, NY: HarperCollins, 1992.

Ehlert, Lois. *Color Farm.* New York, NY: HarperCollins, 1990.

Ehlert, Lois. *Color Zoo.* New York, NY: HarperCollins, 1989.

Ehlert, Lois. *Eating the Alphabet.* Orlando, FL: Harcourt, Brace, Jovanovich, 1989.

Hoban, Tana. *Is It Larger, Is It Smaller?* New York, NY: Greenwillow Books, 1985.

Hoban, Tana. *26 Letters and 99 Cents.* New York, NY: Greenwillow Books, 1987.

McMillan, Bruce. *Beach Ball—Left, Right.* New York, NY: Holiday House, 1992.

McMillan, Bruce. *Eating Fractions.* New York, NY: Scholastic, 1991.

McMillan, Bruce. *Here a Chick, There a Chick.* New York, NY: Lothrop, Lee & Shepard, 1983.

Tactile

Carle, Eric. *The Very Busy Spider.* New York, NY: Philomel, 1985.

Shapes

Carle, Eric. *My Very First Book of Shapes.* New York, NY: HarperCollins, 1991.

Gundersheimer, Karen. *Shapes to Show.* New York, NY: HarperCollins, 1984.

Numbers

Bawden, Juliet and Helen Pask. *Counting Children 1 to 10*. New York, NY: Henry Holt, 1989.

Garne, S. T. *One White Sail*. San Marcos, CA: Green Tiger Press, 1992.

Wordless

McCully, Emily Arnold. *First Snow*. New York, NY: HarperCollins, 1985.

McCully, Emily Arnold. *New Baby*. New York, NY: HarperCollins, 1988.

McCully, Emily Arnold. *Picnic*. New York, NY: HarperCollins, 1984.

McCully, Emily Arnold. *School*. New York, NY: HarperCollins, 1987.

Young, Ed. *The Other Bone*. New York, NY: HarperCollins, 1984.

Songbooks

Jones, Carol. *This Old Man*. Boston, MA: Houghton Mifflin, 1990.

Kovalski, Maryann. *The Wheels on the Bus*. Boston, MA: Little, Brown & Co., 1987.

Poetry

Bryan, Ashley. *Sing to the Sun*. New York, NY: HarperCollins, 1992.

Goldstein, Bobbye S. *Bear in Mind.* New York, NY: Viking Penguin, 1989.

Goldstein, Bobbye S. *Birthday Rhymes, Special Times.* New York, NY: Doubleday, 1993.

Goldstein, Bobbye S. *Inner Chimes: Poems on Poetry.* Honesdale, PA: Boyds Mills Press, 1992.

Goldstein, Bobbye S. *What's on the Menu? Food Poems.* New York, NY: Viking, 1992.

Greenfield, Eloise. *Honey, I Love.* New York, NY: HarperCollins, 1978.

Hoberman, Mary Ann. *A House Is a House for Me.* New York, NY: Viking, 1978.

Hopkins, Lee Bennett. *Good Books, Good Times.* New York, NY: HarperCollins, 1990.

Hopkins, Lee Bennett. *Pterodactlys and Pizza.* New York, NY: The Trumpet Club, 1992.

Prelutsky, Jack. *Beneath the Blue Umbrella.* New York, NY: Greenwillow Books, 1990.

Prelutsky, Jack. *Ride a Purple Pelican.* New York, NY: Greenwillow Books, 1986.

Reference Books

The Random House Children's Encyclopedia. New York, NY: Random House.

The Kingfisher Children's Encyclopedia. New York, NY: Kingfisher Books.

Webster's New World Children's Dictionary. New York, NY: Prentice Hall.

Goldstein, Bobbye S. and Gabriel F. *Newspaper Fun: Activities for Young Children*. Carthage, IL: Fearon Teacher Aids, 1992.

Notes

240